50 Fruit Tart & Galette Recipes for Home

By: Kelly Johnson

Table of Contents

- Classic French Fruit Tart
- Mixed Berry Tart
- Apple Galette
- Lemon Meringue Tart
- Pear and Almond Tart
- Peach Galette
- Strawberry Rhubarb Tart
- Blueberry Lemon Tart
- Apricot Almond Tart
- Plum Tart with Hazelnut Crust
- Raspberry Frangipane Tart
- Fig and Honey Galette
- Cherry Almond Tart
- Pecan and Pear Tart
- Blackberry Lime Tart
- Kiwi and Coconut Tart
- Mango Tart with Pistachio
- Orange and Cream Cheese Tart
- Nectarine Tart
- Passion Fruit Tart
- Cranberry Apple Galette
- Raspberry Peach Tart
- Chocolate Hazelnut Tart
- Chocolate Cherry Galette
- Banana Caramel Tart
- Lemon Lavender Tart
- Grapefruit Tart
- Plum Frangipane Tart
- Apricot and Raspberry Galette
- Pear Frangipane Tart
- Coconut Pineapple Tart
- Lemon Blueberry Tart
- S'mores Fruit Tart
- Mixed Citrus Tart
- Cherry and Almond Galette

- Apple Cranberry Tart
- Spiced Pear Tart
- Strawberry Kiwi Galette
- Apple and Cinnamon Galette
- Blueberry Peach Tart
- Almond Butter Tart with Banana
- Mango Raspberry Galette
- Blackberry Peach Tart
- Tropical Fruit Tart
- Cranberry Pecan Tart
- Coconut Mango Galette
- Strawberry Almond Tart
- Fig and Ricotta Tart
- Lemon Raspberry Galette
- Pear and Chocolate Tart

Classic French Fruit Tart

Ingredients:

- **For the Crust:**
    - 1 ½ cups (180g) all-purpose flour
    - ½ cup (113g) unsalted butter, cold and cubed
    - ¼ cup (50g) sugar
    - 1 egg yolk
    - 1 tablespoon cold water
- **For the Pastry Cream:**
    - 2 cups (480ml) whole milk
    - ½ cup (100g) sugar
    - 4 large egg yolks
    - 1 tablespoon cornstarch
    - 1 teaspoon vanilla extract
- **For the Topping:**
    - 2 cups (300g) mixed fresh fruit (berries, kiwi, etc.)

Instructions:

1. **Prepare the Crust:** Mix flour, butter, and sugar in a food processor. Add egg yolk and water, pulse until dough forms. Chill for 30 minutes, then roll out and line a tart pan.
2. **Bake the Crust:** Preheat oven to 375°F (190°C). Line the crust with parchment and bake for 20 minutes, then remove the paper and bake for another 5 minutes.
3. **Make the Pastry Cream:** Whisk together egg yolks, sugar, and cornstarch in a bowl. Heat milk in a saucepan until hot, then slowly pour it into the egg mixture. Return to the pan, cook until thickened, then stir in vanilla. Let cool.
4. **Assemble the Tart:** Spread pastry cream into the cooled crust, arrange the fruit on top, and refrigerate before serving.

Mixed Berry Tart

Ingredients:

- **For the Crust:**
    - 1 ½ cups (180g) all-purpose flour
    - ½ cup (113g) unsalted butter, cubed
    - ¼ cup (50g) sugar
    - 1 egg yolk
- **For the Filling:**
    - 2 cups (300g) mixed berries (strawberries, raspberries, blackberries)
    - 1 cup (240ml) heavy cream
    - ½ cup (50g) sugar
    - 1 teaspoon vanilla extract

Instructions:

1. **Prepare the Crust:** Combine flour, butter, sugar, and egg yolk. Form dough, chill for 30 minutes, roll out, and line a tart pan.
2. **Bake the Crust:** Preheat oven to 375°F (190°C). Line the tart shell with parchment and bake for 20 minutes, then remove parchment and bake for another 5 minutes.
3. **Make the Filling:** Whisk heavy cream, sugar, and vanilla until stiff peaks form.
4. **Assemble the Tart:** Spread whipped cream over the cooled tart shell and top with fresh mixed berries.

Apple Galette

Ingredients:

- **For the Crust:**
    - 1 ¼ cups (150g) all-purpose flour
    - ¼ cup (50g) sugar
    - ½ cup (113g) unsalted butter, cubed
    - 1 egg yolk
    - 2 tablespoons cold water
- **For the Filling:**
    - 4 apples, peeled and sliced
    - ¼ cup (50g) sugar
    - 1 teaspoon cinnamon
    - 1 tablespoon lemon juice

Instructions:

1. **Prepare the Crust:** Mix flour, sugar, and butter in a food processor. Add egg yolk and cold water, pulse until dough forms. Chill for 30 minutes.
2. **Prepare the Filling:** Toss sliced apples with sugar, cinnamon, and lemon juice.
3. **Assemble the Galette:** Roll out dough, arrange apples in the center, and fold the edges over. Bake at 375°F (190°C) for 35-40 minutes.

Lemon Meringue Tart

Ingredients:

- **For the Crust:**
    - 1 ½ cups (180g) all-purpose flour
    - ½ cup (113g) unsalted butter, cubed
    - ¼ cup (50g) sugar
    - 1 egg yolk
- **For the Filling:**
    - 1 cup (240ml) fresh lemon juice
    - 1 cup (200g) sugar
    - 4 large egg yolks
    - 2 tablespoons cornstarch
    - 1 tablespoon unsalted butter
- **For the Meringue:**
    - 4 large egg whites
    - ¼ cup (50g) sugar

Instructions:

1. **Prepare the Crust:** Combine flour, butter, sugar, and egg yolk. Form dough, chill, then roll out and bake at 375°F (190°C) for 20-25 minutes.
2. **Make the Filling:** Whisk together lemon juice, sugar, egg yolks, cornstarch, and cook over medium heat until thickened. Stir in butter.
3. **Make the Meringue:** Beat egg whites with sugar until stiff peaks form.
4. **Assemble the Tart:** Pour lemon filling into the crust, top with meringue, and bake at 350°F (175°C) for 10-12 minutes until golden.

Pear and Almond Tart

Ingredients:

- **For the Crust:**
    - 1 ½ cups (180g) all-purpose flour
    - ½ cup (113g) unsalted butter, cubed
    - ¼ cup (50g) sugar
    - 1 egg yolk
- **For the Filling:**
    - 2 pears, peeled and sliced
    - ½ cup (50g) almond flour
    - ¼ cup (50g) sugar
    - 1 teaspoon almond extract

Instructions:

1. **Prepare the Crust:** Mix flour, butter, sugar, and egg yolk. Chill for 30 minutes, roll out, and line a tart pan.
2. **Prepare the Filling:** Mix almond flour, sugar, and almond extract. Spread over the crust, then arrange pear slices on top.
3. **Bake:** Bake at 375°F (190°C) for 35-40 minutes until golden.

Peach Galette

Ingredients:

- **For the Crust:**
    - 1 ¼ cups (150g) all-purpose flour
    - ½ cup (113g) unsalted butter, cubed
    - ¼ cup (50g) sugar
    - 2 tablespoons cold water
- **For the Filling:**
    - 4 ripe peaches, peeled and sliced
    - ¼ cup (50g) sugar
    - 1 teaspoon cinnamon

Instructions:

1. **Prepare the Crust:** Combine flour, butter, and sugar in a food processor. Add cold water, pulse to form dough, and chill for 30 minutes.
2. **Prepare the Filling:** Toss peach slices with sugar and cinnamon.
3. **Assemble the Galette:** Roll out dough, place peach mixture in the center, and fold the edges over. Bake at 375°F (190°C) for 30-35 minutes.

Strawberry Rhubarb Tart

Ingredients:

- **For the Crust:**
    - 1 ½ cups (180g) all-purpose flour
    - ½ cup (113g) unsalted butter, cubed
    - ¼ cup (50g) sugar
    - 1 egg yolk
- **For the Filling:**
    - 1 cup (150g) fresh strawberries, sliced
    - 1 cup (150g) rhubarb, chopped
    - ½ cup (100g) sugar
    - 2 tablespoons cornstarch

Instructions:

1. **Prepare the Crust:** Mix flour, butter, sugar, and egg yolk to form dough. Chill, then roll out and line a tart pan.
2. **Prepare the Filling:** Toss strawberries, rhubarb, sugar, and cornstarch together.
3. **Bake:** Pour filling into the crust and bake at 375°F (190°C) for 35-40 minutes.

Blueberry Lemon Tart

Ingredients:

- **For the Crust:**
    - 1 ½ cups (180g) all-purpose flour
    - ½ cup (113g) unsalted butter, cubed
    - ¼ cup (50g) sugar
    - 1 egg yolk
- **For the Filling:**
    - 1 ½ cups (225g) fresh blueberries
    - ½ cup (100g) sugar
    - 2 large eggs
    - 2 tablespoons lemon juice
    - 1 teaspoon lemon zest

Instructions:

1. **Prepare the Crust:** Mix flour, butter, sugar, and egg yolk. Roll out, chill, and bake at 375°F (190°C) for 20-25 minutes.
2. **Prepare the Filling:** Whisk together eggs, sugar, lemon juice, and zest, then fold in blueberries.
3. **Bake:** Pour filling into the crust and bake for 20-25 minutes until set.

Apricot Almond Tart

Ingredients:

- **For the Crust:**
    - 1 ½ cups (180g) all-purpose flour
    - ½ cup (113g) unsalted butter, cubed
    - ¼ cup (50g) sugar
    - 1 egg yolk
- **For the Filling:**
    - 1 cup (150g) apricot preserves
    - ½ cup (50g) almond flour
    - ¼ cup (50g) sugar
    - 1 teaspoon vanilla extract

Instructions:

1. **Prepare the Crust:** Mix flour, butter, sugar, and egg yolk to form dough. Chill, then roll out and line a tart pan.
2. **Prepare the Filling:** Mix almond flour, sugar, and vanilla, then spread apricot preserves on the crust.
3. **Assemble & Bake:** Add almond mixture on top of preserves, and bake at 375°F (190°C) for 25-30 minutes.

Plum Tart with Hazelnut Crust

Ingredients:

- **For the Crust:**
    - 1 cup (120g) all-purpose flour
    - ½ cup (60g) ground hazelnuts
    - ¼ cup (50g) sugar
    - ½ cup (113g) unsalted butter, cubed
    - 1 egg yolk
- **For the Filling:**
    - 4 ripe plums, sliced
    - ¼ cup (50g) sugar
    - 1 teaspoon cinnamon
    - 1 tablespoon cornstarch

Instructions:

1. **Prepare the Crust:** Combine flour, hazelnuts, sugar, and butter in a food processor. Add egg yolk and pulse until dough forms. Chill for 30 minutes.
2. **Prepare the Filling:** Toss plums with sugar, cinnamon, and cornstarch.
3. **Assemble & Bake:** Roll out dough, place into tart pan, add filling, and bake at 375°F (190°C) for 30-35 minutes.

Raspberry Frangipane Tart

Ingredients:

- **For the Crust:**
    - 1 ½ cups (180g) all-purpose flour
    - ½ cup (113g) unsalted butter, cubed
    - ¼ cup (50g) sugar
    - 1 egg yolk
- **For the Frangipane Filling:**
    - ½ cup (113g) unsalted butter, softened
    - ½ cup (100g) sugar
    - 1 cup (100g) almond flour
    - 1 large egg
    - 1 teaspoon almond extract
- **For the Topping:**
    - 1 cup (150g) fresh raspberries

Instructions:

1. **Prepare the Crust:** Mix flour, butter, sugar, and egg yolk. Chill, then roll out and line a tart pan. Bake at 375°F (190°C) for 20 minutes.
2. **Make the Frangipane:** Beat butter and sugar, add almond flour, egg, and almond extract. Spread over baked crust.
3. **Bake & Finish:** Arrange raspberries on top and bake for another 20-25 minutes until golden.

Fig and Honey Galette

Ingredients:

- **For the Crust:**
    - 1 ¼ cups (150g) all-purpose flour
    - ½ cup (113g) unsalted butter, cubed
    - ¼ cup (50g) sugar
    - 2 tablespoons cold water
- **For the Filling:**
    - 6 fresh figs, sliced
    - ¼ cup (60ml) honey
    - ½ teaspoon cinnamon

Instructions:

1. **Prepare the Crust:** Mix flour, butter, and sugar. Add water, pulse to form dough, and chill for 30 minutes.
2. **Prepare the Filling:** Toss figs with honey and cinnamon.
3. **Assemble & Bake:** Roll out dough, arrange figs in the center, fold edges over, and bake at 375°F (190°C) for 30 minutes.

Cherry Almond Tart

Ingredients:

- **For the Crust:**
    - 1 ½ cups (180g) all-purpose flour
    - ½ cup (113g) unsalted butter, cubed
    - ¼ cup (50g) sugar
    - 1 egg yolk
- **For the Filling:**
    - 2 cups (300g) fresh cherries, pitted
    - ½ cup (50g) almond flour
    - ¼ cup (50g) sugar
    - 1 teaspoon almond extract

Instructions:

1. **Prepare the Crust:** Mix flour, butter, sugar, and egg yolk. Roll out, chill, and pre-bake at 375°F (190°C) for 20 minutes.
2. **Prepare the Filling:** Toss cherries with sugar, almond flour, and almond extract.
3. **Assemble & Bake:** Spread filling into crust and bake for 30 minutes.

Pecan and Pear Tart

Ingredients:

- **For the Crust:**
    - 1 ½ cups (180g) all-purpose flour
    - ½ cup (113g) unsalted butter
    - ¼ cup (50g) sugar
    - 1 egg yolk
- **For the Filling:**
    - 2 pears, sliced
    - ½ cup (60g) chopped pecans
    - ¼ cup (50g) sugar
    - 1 teaspoon vanilla extract

Instructions:

1. **Prepare the Crust:** Mix flour, butter, sugar, and egg yolk. Chill, then roll out and bake at 375°F (190°C) for 20 minutes.
2. **Prepare the Filling:** Toss pears with sugar, vanilla, and pecans.
3. **Bake:** Pour filling into crust and bake for another 25 minutes.

Blackberry Lime Tart

Ingredients:

- 1 ½ cups (180g) all-purpose flour
- ½ cup (113g) unsalted butter
- ¼ cup (50g) sugar
- 2 cups (300g) fresh blackberries
- 2 tablespoons lime juice
- 1 teaspoon lime zest

Instructions:

1. Prepare the crust and pre-bake.
2. Toss blackberries with lime juice, zest, and sugar.
3. Fill the crust and bake for 25 minutes at 375°F (190°C).

Kiwi and Coconut Tart

Ingredients:

- 1 ½ cups (180g) flour
- ½ cup (113g) butter
- ¼ cup (50g) sugar
- 2 cups (300g) sliced kiwi
- ½ cup (50g) shredded coconut

Instructions:

1. Prepare and bake crust.
2. Sprinkle coconut over crust and top with kiwi slices.
3. Bake for 20 minutes at 350°F (175°C).

Mango Tart with Pistachio

Ingredients:

- 1 ½ cups (180g) flour
- ½ cup (113g) butter
- ¼ cup (50g) sugar
- 2 ripe mangoes, sliced
- ¼ cup (30g) chopped pistachios

Instructions:

1. Prepare and bake crust.
2. Arrange mango slices and sprinkle pistachios on top.
3. Bake for 20 minutes at 350°F (175°C).

Orange and Cream Cheese Tart

Ingredients:

- 1 ½ cups (180g) flour
- ½ cup (113g) butter
- ¼ cup (50g) sugar
- 8oz (225g) cream cheese
- ¼ cup (60ml) honey
- 2 oranges, sliced

Instructions:

1. Prepare and bake crust.
2. Mix cream cheese with honey, spread over crust, and top with oranges.
3. Bake for 20 minutes at 350°F (175°C).

Nectarine Tart

Ingredients:

- 1 ½ cups (180g) flour
- ½ cup (113g) butter
- ¼ cup (50g) sugar
- 3 nectarines, sliced

Instructions:

1. Prepare and bake crust.
2. Arrange nectarines and bake for 30 minutes at 375°F (190°C).

Passion Fruit Tart

Ingredients:

- 1 ½ cups (180g) flour
- ½ cup (113g) butter
- ¼ cup (50g) sugar
- ½ cup (120ml) passion fruit pulp
- ½ cup (120ml) heavy cream

Instructions:

1. Prepare and bake crust.
2. Mix passion fruit pulp with cream and sugar, pour into crust.
3. Chill before serving.

Cranberry Apple Galette

Ingredients:

- **For the Crust:**
    - 1 ¼ cups (150g) all-purpose flour
    - ½ cup (113g) unsalted butter, cubed
    - ¼ cup (50g) sugar
    - 2 tablespoons cold water
- **For the Filling:**
    - 2 apples, peeled and sliced
    - ½ cup (75g) fresh cranberries
    - ¼ cup (50g) sugar
    - 1 teaspoon cinnamon
    - 1 tablespoon cornstarch

Instructions:

1. **Prepare the Crust:** Mix flour, butter, and sugar. Add water, form a dough, chill for 30 minutes.
2. **Prepare the Filling:** Toss apples, cranberries, sugar, cinnamon, and cornstarch.
3. **Assemble & Bake:** Roll out dough, place filling in the center, fold edges over, and bake at 375°F (190°C) for 35 minutes.

Raspberry Peach Tart

Ingredients:

- **For the Crust:**
    - 1 ½ cups (180g) all-purpose flour
    - ½ cup (113g) unsalted butter, cubed
    - ¼ cup (50g) sugar
    - 1 egg yolk
- **For the Filling:**
    - 2 peaches, sliced
    - 1 cup (150g) raspberries
    - ¼ cup (50g) sugar
    - 1 tablespoon cornstarch

Instructions:

1. **Prepare & Bake the Crust.**
2. **Prepare the Filling:** Toss peaches, raspberries, sugar, and cornstarch.
3. **Bake:** Pour into crust and bake at 375°F (190°C) for 30 minutes.

Chocolate Hazelnut Tart

Ingredients:

- **For the Crust:**
    - 1 ¼ cups (150g) all-purpose flour
    - ¼ cup (25g) cocoa powder
    - ½ cup (113g) butter
- **For the Filling:**
    - ½ cup (120ml) heavy cream
    - ½ cup (100g) dark chocolate, chopped
    - ¼ cup (50g) hazelnut butter

Instructions:

1. **Prepare & Bake the Crust.**
2. **Prepare the Filling:** Heat cream, pour over chocolate, stir in hazelnut butter.
3. **Chill:** Pour into crust and refrigerate for 2 hours before serving.

Chocolate Cherry Galette

Ingredients:

- **For the Crust:**
    - 1 ¼ cups (150g) all-purpose flour
    - ¼ cup (25g) cocoa powder
    - ½ cup (113g) butter
- **For the Filling:**
    - 1 ½ cups (225g) cherries, pitted
    - ¼ cup (50g) sugar
    - 1 tablespoon cornstarch

Instructions:

1. **Prepare & Chill Dough.**
2. **Prepare Filling:** Toss cherries with sugar and cornstarch.
3. **Assemble & Bake:** Roll out dough, place cherries in center, fold edges, and bake at 375°F (190°C) for 35 minutes.

Banana Caramel Tart

Ingredients:

- **For the Crust:**
    - 1 ½ cups (180g) all-purpose flour
    - ½ cup (113g) unsalted butter
    - ¼ cup (50g) sugar
- **For the Filling:**
    - 2 bananas, sliced
    - ½ cup (120ml) caramel sauce
    - ½ cup (120ml) heavy cream

Instructions:

1. **Prepare & Bake the Crust.**
2. **Prepare the Filling:** Spread caramel in crust, layer with bananas, and top with whipped cream.

Lemon Lavender Tart

Ingredients:

- **For the Crust:**
    - 1 ½ cups (180g) all-purpose flour
    - ½ cup (113g) butter
    - ¼ cup (50g) sugar
- **For the Filling:**
    - 1 cup (240ml) lemon juice
    - ½ cup (100g) sugar
    - 1 teaspoon dried lavender
    - 2 tablespoons cornstarch
    - 2 eggs

Instructions:

1. **Prepare & Bake the Crust.**
2. **Prepare the Filling:** Whisk lemon juice, sugar, lavender, cornstarch, and eggs, then cook until thick.
3. **Chill:** Pour into crust and refrigerate for 2 hours.

Grapefruit Tart

Ingredients:

- **For the Crust:**
    - 1 ½ cups (180g) all-purpose flour
    - ½ cup (113g) butter
    - ¼ cup (50g) sugar
- **For the Filling:**
    - 1 cup (240ml) grapefruit juice
    - ½ cup (100g) sugar
    - 2 tablespoons cornstarch
    - 2 eggs

Instructions:

1. **Prepare & Bake the Crust.**
2. **Prepare the Filling:** Whisk grapefruit juice, sugar, cornstarch, and eggs, cook until thick.
3. **Chill:** Pour into crust and refrigerate before serving.

Plum Frangipane Tart

Ingredients:

- **For the Crust:**
    - 1 ½ cups (180g) all-purpose flour
    - ½ cup (113g) butter
- **For the Filling:**
    - ½ cup (113g) butter
    - ½ cup (100g) sugar
    - 1 cup (100g) almond flour
    - 1 egg
    - 2 plums, sliced

Instructions:

1. **Prepare & Bake the Crust.**
2. **Prepare Frangipane:** Beat butter, sugar, almond flour, and egg, spread in crust.
3. **Bake:** Top with plums and bake at 375°F (190°C) for 30 minutes.

Apricot and Raspberry Galette

Ingredients:

- **For the Crust:**
    - 1 ¼ cups (150g) flour
    - ½ cup (113g) butter
- **For the Filling:**
    - 3 apricots, sliced
    - ½ cup (75g) raspberries
    - ¼ cup (50g) sugar
    - 1 tablespoon cornstarch

Instructions:

1. **Prepare & Chill Dough.**
2. **Prepare Filling:** Toss fruit with sugar and cornstarch.
3. **Assemble & Bake:** Roll out dough, place filling in center, fold edges, and bake at 375°F (190°C) for 35 minutes.

Pear Frangipane Tart

Ingredients:

- **For the Crust:**
    - 1 ½ cups (180g) all-purpose flour
    - ½ cup (113g) butter
- **For the Filling:**
    - ½ cup (113g) butter
    - ½ cup (100g) sugar
    - 1 cup (100g) almond flour
    - 1 egg
    - 2 pears, sliced

Instructions:

1. **Prepare & Bake the Crust.**
2. **Prepare Frangipane:** Beat butter, sugar, almond flour, and egg, spread in crust.
3. **Bake:** Top with pears and bake at 375°F (190°C) for 30 minutes.

Coconut Pineapple Tart

Ingredients:

- **For the Crust:**
    - 1 ½ cups (180g) all-purpose flour
    - ½ cup (113g) unsalted butter, cubed
    - ¼ cup (50g) sugar
    - 1 egg yolk
- **For the Filling:**
    - 1 cup (240ml) coconut milk
    - ½ cup (120g) crushed pineapple
    - ¼ cup (50g) sugar
    - 2 tablespoons cornstarch
    - ½ teaspoon vanilla extract

Instructions:

1. **Prepare & Bake the Crust.**
2. **Make the Filling:** Heat coconut milk, pineapple, sugar, and cornstarch in a saucepan until thickened.
3. **Assemble & Chill:** Pour filling into crust and refrigerate for at least 2 hours.

Lemon Blueberry Tart

Ingredients:

- **For the Crust:** *(same as above)*
- **For the Filling:**
    - 1 cup (240ml) fresh lemon juice
    - ½ cup (100g) sugar
    - 2 eggs
    - 2 tablespoons cornstarch
    - 1 teaspoon lemon zest
    - 1 cup (150g) fresh blueberries

Instructions:

1. **Prepare & Bake the Crust.**
2. **Prepare the Filling:** Whisk lemon juice, sugar, eggs, cornstarch, and zest, cook until thick.
3. **Assemble & Bake:** Pour into crust, top with blueberries, and bake at 350°F (175°C) for 15 minutes.

S'mores Fruit Tart

Ingredients:

- **For the Crust:**
    - 1 ½ cups (180g) graham cracker crumbs
    - ½ cup (113g) melted butter
- **For the Filling:**
    - 1 cup (175g) chopped strawberries
    - ½ cup (75g) blueberries
    - ½ cup (120ml) melted dark chocolate
    - 1 cup (50g) mini marshmallows

Instructions:

1. **Prepare & Bake the Crust:** Mix crumbs and butter, press into tart pan, bake at 350°F (175°C) for 10 minutes.
2. **Assemble:** Spread melted chocolate, add fruit, top with marshmallows.
3. **Torch Marshmallows:** Lightly toast with a kitchen torch.

Mixed Citrus Tart

Ingredients:

- **For the Crust:** *(same as above)*
- **For the Filling:**
    - 1 cup (240ml) orange juice
    - ½ cup (120ml) grapefruit juice
    - ½ cup (100g) sugar
    - 2 tablespoons cornstarch
    - Zest from one lemon, lime, and orange

Instructions:

1. **Prepare & Bake the Crust.**
2. **Prepare the Filling:** Whisk juices, sugar, cornstarch, and zest, cook until thickened.
3. **Assemble & Chill:** Pour into crust and refrigerate for at least 2 hours.

Cherry and Almond Galette

Ingredients:

- **For the Crust:** *(same as above)*
- **For the Filling:**
    - 2 cups (300g) cherries, pitted
    - ¼ cup (50g) sugar
    - 1 teaspoon almond extract
    - ¼ cup (30g) sliced almonds

Instructions:

1. **Prepare & Chill Dough.**
2. **Prepare Filling:** Toss cherries with sugar and almond extract.
3. **Assemble & Bake:** Roll out dough, place cherries in center, fold edges, sprinkle with almonds, and bake at 375°F (190°C) for 35 minutes.

Apple Cranberry Tart

Ingredients:

- **For the Crust:** *(same as above)*
- **For the Filling:**
    - 2 apples, sliced
    - ½ cup (75g) fresh cranberries
    - ¼ cup (50g) sugar
    - 1 teaspoon cinnamon

Instructions:

1. **Prepare & Bake the Crust.**
2. **Prepare Filling:** Toss apples, cranberries, sugar, and cinnamon.
3. **Bake:** Pour filling into crust and bake at 375°F (190°C) for 30 minutes.

Spiced Pear Tart

Ingredients:

- **For the Crust:** *(same as above)*
- **For the Filling:**
    - 2 pears, sliced
    - ¼ cup (50g) sugar
    - 1 teaspoon cinnamon
    - ¼ teaspoon nutmeg

Instructions:

1. **Prepare & Bake the Crust.**
2. **Prepare the Filling:** Toss pears, sugar, cinnamon, and nutmeg.
3. **Bake:** Pour filling into crust and bake at 375°F (190°C) for 30 minutes.

Strawberry Kiwi Galette

Ingredients:

- **For the Crust:** *(same as above)*
- **For the Filling:**
    - 2 cups (300g) sliced strawberries
    - 2 kiwis, sliced
    - ¼ cup (50g) sugar

Instructions:

1. **Prepare & Chill Dough.**
2. **Prepare Filling:** Toss fruit with sugar.
3. **Assemble & Bake:** Roll out dough, place filling in center, fold edges, and bake at 375°F (190°C) for 30 minutes.

Apple and Cinnamon Galette

Ingredients:

- **For the Crust:** *(same as above)*
- **For the Filling:**
    - 2 apples, sliced
    - ¼ cup (50g) sugar
    - 1 teaspoon cinnamon

Instructions:

1. **Prepare & Chill Dough.**
2. **Prepare Filling:** Toss apples, sugar, and cinnamon.
3. **Assemble & Bake:** Roll out dough, place apples in center, fold edges, and bake at 375°F (190°C) for 30 minutes.

Blueberry Peach Tart

Ingredients:

- **For the Crust:** *(same as above)*
- **For the Filling:**
    - 2 peaches, sliced
    - 1 cup (150g) blueberries
    - ¼ cup (50g) sugar

Instructions:

1. **Prepare & Bake the Crust.**
2. **Prepare Filling:** Toss peaches, blueberries, and sugar.
3. **Bake:** Pour into crust and bake at 375°F (190°C) for 30 minutes.

Almond Butter Tart with Banana

Ingredients:

- **For the Crust:** *(same as above)*
- **For the Filling:**
    - ½ cup (120g) almond butter
    - 2 bananas, sliced
    - ¼ cup (50g) honey

Instructions:

1. **Prepare & Bake the Crust.**
2. **Prepare Filling:** Spread almond butter over crust, top with banana slices, drizzle with honey.
3. **Chill:** Refrigerate for at least 1 hour before serving.

Mango Raspberry Galette

Ingredients:

- **For the Crust:**
    - 1 ¼ cups (150g) all-purpose flour
    - ½ cup (113g) unsalted butter, cubed
    - ¼ cup (50g) sugar
    - 2 tablespoons cold water
- **For the Filling:**
    - 1 cup (150g) fresh mango, diced
    - ½ cup (75g) fresh raspberries
    - ¼ cup (50g) sugar
    - 1 tablespoon cornstarch

Instructions:

1. **Prepare & Chill Dough.**
2. **Prepare Filling:** Toss mango, raspberries, sugar, and cornstarch.
3. **Assemble & Bake:** Roll out dough, place filling in center, fold edges, and bake at 375°F (190°C) for 35 minutes.

Blackberry Peach Tart

Ingredients:

- **For the Crust:** *(same as above)*
- **For the Filling:**
    - 2 peaches, sliced
    - 1 cup (150g) blackberries
    - ¼ cup (50g) sugar
    - 1 tablespoon lemon juice

Instructions:

1. **Prepare & Bake the Crust.**
2. **Prepare the Filling:** Toss peaches, blackberries, sugar, and lemon juice.
3. **Bake:** Pour filling into crust and bake at 375°F (190°C) for 30 minutes.

Tropical Fruit Tart

Ingredients:

- **For the Crust:** *(same as above)*
- **For the Filling:**
    - ½ cup (120ml) coconut milk
    - 1 tablespoon cornstarch
    - ½ cup (75g) chopped pineapple
    - ½ cup (75g) diced mango
    - ¼ cup (50g) shredded coconut

Instructions:

1. **Prepare & Bake the Crust.**
2. **Prepare the Filling:** Heat coconut milk and cornstarch until thickened, then mix in pineapple and mango.
3. **Assemble & Chill:** Pour into crust, top with shredded coconut, and refrigerate before serving.

Cranberry Pecan Tart

Ingredients:

- **For the Crust:** *(same as above)*
- **For the Filling:**
    - 1 cup (100g) pecans, chopped
    - ½ cup (75g) cranberries
    - ¼ cup (60ml) maple syrup
    - 1 tablespoon cornstarch

Instructions:

1. **Prepare & Bake the Crust.**
2. **Prepare the Filling:** Toss pecans and cranberries with maple syrup and cornstarch.
3. **Bake:** Pour into crust and bake at 350°F (175°C) for 25 minutes.

Coconut Mango Galette

Ingredients:

- **For the Crust:** *(same as above)*
- **For the Filling:**
    - 1 cup (150g) fresh mango, sliced
    - ¼ cup (50g) shredded coconut
    - ¼ cup (50g) sugar

Instructions:

1. **Prepare & Chill Dough.**
2. **Prepare the Filling:** Toss mango and coconut with sugar.
3. **Assemble & Bake:** Roll out dough, place filling in center, fold edges, and bake at 375°F (190°C) for 30 minutes.

Strawberry Almond Tart

Ingredients:

- **For the Crust:** *(same as above)*
- **For the Filling:**
    - 1 cup (150g) fresh strawberries, sliced
    - ½ cup (50g) almond flour
    - ¼ cup (50g) sugar
    - 1 teaspoon almond extract

Instructions:

1. **Prepare & Bake the Crust.**
2. **Prepare the Filling:** Toss strawberries, almond flour, sugar, and almond extract.
3. **Bake:** Pour into crust and bake at 375°F (190°C) for 30 minutes.

Fig and Ricotta Tart

Ingredients:

- **For the Crust:** *(same as above)*
- **For the Filling:**
    - ½ cup (120g) ricotta cheese
    - 1 tablespoon honey
    - 4 fresh figs, sliced

Instructions:

1. **Prepare & Bake the Crust.**
2. **Prepare the Filling:** Mix ricotta with honey and spread over crust.
3. **Assemble & Chill:** Top with figs and refrigerate for 1 hour.

Lemon Raspberry Galette

Ingredients:

- **For the Crust:** *(same as above)*
- **For the Filling:**
    - 1 cup (150g) fresh raspberries
    - ¼ cup (50g) sugar
    - 1 tablespoon lemon zest
    - 1 tablespoon cornstarch

Instructions:

1. **Prepare & Chill Dough.**
2. **Prepare the Filling:** Toss raspberries with sugar, lemon zest, and cornstarch.
3. **Assemble & Bake:** Roll out dough, place filling in center, fold edges, and bake at 375°F (190°C) for 30 minutes.

Pear and Chocolate Tart

Ingredients:

- **For the Crust:** *(same as above)*
- **For the Filling:**
    - 2 pears, sliced
    - ½ cup (100g) dark chocolate, melted
    - ¼ cup (50g) sugar

Instructions:

1. **Prepare & Bake the Crust.**
2. **Prepare the Filling:** Spread melted chocolate over crust, arrange pears on top, and sprinkle with sugar.
3. **Bake:** Bake at 375°F (190°C) for 25 minutes.

www.ingramcontent.com/pod-product-compliance
Lightning Source LLC
LaVergne TN
LVHW081337060526
838201LV00055B/2711